FAIR ISLE'S
'GARDEN' BIRDS

D1422713

FAIR ISLE'S 'GARDEN' BIRDS

by John Holloway

The Shetland Times Ltd.
Lerwick
1984

First published 1984

© John Holloway, 1983

ISBN 0 900662 39 5

Title page illustration: Pallas's Warbler

Printed and published by
The Shetland Times Ltd.,
Prince Alfred Street, Lerwick, Shetland.

CONTENTS

Introduction   7

About the author   9

Part I   A diary of the birds seen from the Fair Isle Shop
            between February 1978 and February 1983. 37
            coloured plates with text   11

Part II   'Garden' birds seen by the author elsewhere on
            the isle. 23 coloured plates with text   87

Part III   Ornithological recollections as told by each of
            the Fair Isle households. A sketch of each house
            accompanies the text   135

Map of Fair Isle   154

Acknowledgments   156

Index   157

STACKHOULL

INTRODUCTION

To the ornithologist, Fair Isle really is something special. Several of the species we have seen in our garden are not even depicted in many of the British bird-books. Where else in Great Britain could one expect to look out of the bedroom window and see an Olive-backed Pipit striding about the grass, or look out of the kitchen window and see a Little Bunting feeding with the local sparrows? Well, that is Fair Isle — 'Mecca' to the ornithologist.

Our first thoughts when we came to the isle were how to make the garden as attractive to birds as possible and we completely redesigned it, building up old walls and erecting new ones. A few boot-loads of cuttings of the hardy rose which flourishes in certain places on the isle and we were on our way. A compost heap at the back of the house and a pile of rotting fruit in the front garden and the job was just about complete. It has certainly worked and, including birds flying over, our 'garden list' now stands at 177. Part I of this book is a personal diary of the species we have seen in the five years since February 1978. Lack of space has prevented me from illustrating all the species we have seen and I have therefore generally chosen to depict the rarer or more interesting ones. I make no apology for the lack of elaborate backgrounds to the illustrations; it would be impossible for me to do the isle justice, so if you've not already been to Fair Isle — come and see for yourselves.

Part II is a selection of some of the rarer species I have seen elsewhere on the isle, with emphasis on what could loosely be termed 'garden' birds. I hope that this section will be of some value as a guide to some of the rarer species, particularly those which are seen on Fair Isle with amazing regularity and yet are hardly ever seen elsewhere in Britain.

Part III, the final section, contains a contribution from each of the Fair Isle households and makes interesting and often humorous reading to the ornithologist.

Why is Fair Isle so special to the ornithologist? Size plays a great part. There is always the chance that a rare species will be easy to locate on so small an island. The number of birdwatchers per acre is another important factor. Having said that, the number of species which are seen once and then defy all subsequent attempts to locate them is remarkable and lends weight to my own feelings that luck plays a major part in the discovery of a particular bird. The Great Bustard feather found in 1979 is a classic example of 'the one that got away'. Our children have all helped to add species to our 'garden' list. Hazel spotted our first Crossbill — on the chimney-pot; Hayden found our first Siskins and Kevin flushed our only 'garden' Corncrake while playing outside in the garden. We told him what the bird was he had almost trodden on and he replied — "That Cornflake frightened me!" Without doubt the odds of finding a rare bird on Fair Isle are shorter than anywhere else in Britain.

One thing has become patently obvious since we came to Fair Isle and that is that it is not worth dashing off at dawn in search of newly arrived birds. Birds may arrive on the isle at any time of day. After all, a lost migrant probably doesn't even know that Fair Isle exists and in any case is at the mercy of the elements. How many times I have been out early in the morning and seen nothing, and then gone out later in the day to find birds everywhere! The two species I have added to the island list, Roller and Red Kite, were both discovered after mid-day.

Another fact has also become clear; birds may be found at any part of the island. Although we tend to concentrate on the crofting area, some of the rarest birds turn up in such places as the garage at the north lighthouse, the top of Ward Hill, or self-caught in one of the catching boxes of the Heligoland traps. There certainly is no norm for the habitat of a lost migrant.

It is quite amazing that new species are added to the island list year after year. And who knows what the next five years have "in store"!

Keep ticking!

John F. Holloway,
Stackhoull Stores,
Fair Isle, 1983

THE AUTHOR

Although a Yorkshireman by birth, John Holloway spent much of his early life in Gillingham, Kent. After giving up a career in the civil service to do a job which suited his love for sport and the great outdoors, he ran the local outdoor swimming pool before moving to Orkney in 1977. Later that year John, his wife Sue, and Hazel and Hayden, their two children, (now three with the addition of Kevin) moved to Fair Isle to take over the island shop.

A keen footballer — John turned down several offers to turn semi-professional — it had long been in his mind to move North once his playing days were over and devote more time to his other love, ornithology.

Much of John's time as a boy was spent on a farm near Leeds where his interest in birds began and, on moving to Kent in 1954 this interest was further kindled when he found a dead Wryneck at what, he was later to find out, was their last stronghold in Britain.

A cartographer by profession, it is only since moving to Fair Isle that John has been able to exploit his talent as an artist and he now spends much of his time working on commissions.

A regular visitor to Cley, Norfolk, in the late fifties and early sixties, John first visited Fair Isle in 1966 and his tenth visit in 1977 was to take over the island shop.

Part I

A diary of birds seen in and around Stackhoull Garden
during the five years from February 1978
to February 1983.

Birds underlined in the text are illustrated on the plate
opposite and the date of our first sighting
is recorded alongside each species.

1978

House Sparrow (5¾")   4th February

What else could our first bird be? We can, however, thank the local sparrows for attracting many of the rarer species to the garden. It is quite common for finches and buntings to join the local flock of feeding sparrows.

Fulmar (18½")   4th February

If we look outside and can't see one, we know we are away on holiday!

Song Thrush (9")   4th February

Not such a garden bird on Fair Isle as elsewhere, although we do see them on the lawn occasionally searching for worms, as was our first one.

Snow Bunting (6½")   4th February

Odd birds visit the garden, particularly on spring migration. A nice male landed on the garden wall as we moved in.

Shag (30")   4th February

Can always be seen flying to and from the west cliffs where they nest.

Blackbird (10")   4th February

One of the few passerines that regularly winter on the isle, as the first we saw — ringed — surely had.

Redwing (8¼")   4th February

The lone bird we saw on our first day looked a little lost compared to the 60 or so we had in the garden on 14th October, 1979, when 65,000 were on the isle.

Carrion/Hooded Crow (18½")   4th February

A pair just outside the garden as we unloaded our furniture. A very wary visitor to the scraps.

House Sparrow

Snow Bunting

Hooded Crow

Raven (25″)   4th February

Even the hardy Raven visits the garden occasionally, but always in the snow when carrion is in short supply. Our first sighting was a pair flying over, calling.

Fieldfare (10″)   4th February

One seen as we moved in. A regular garden bird on migration and we have even heard birds singing in spring.

Rock Dove (13″)   4th February

Fair Isle's Rock Doves are still of truly wild strain and very unapproachable. Odd birds seem to forget and come to the garden to feed and 30 in the front garden in late autumn 1982 was exceptional. Our first were a pair flying over.

Rock Pipit (6½″)   4th February

Almost exclusively a bird of the coastline, although a few winter inland. One paid the garden a brief visit on our first day.

Herring Gull (22″)   4th February

Generally the most common gull on the island and a flock of gulls east of the shop as we moved in was predominantly of this species.

Glaucous Gull (27″)   4th February

The best bird on our first day at Stackhoull. A first-winter bird flew over. We have seen birds in all plumages flying over since, but none have dropped in — yet!

Turnstone (9″)   4th February

We watched a flock feeding in the field opposite the shop as we moved in and one enterprising bird actually came in and fed at the scraps in January 1979.

Starling (8½″)   4th February

Yes, they're even here, and if anything even more greedy!

Great Black-backed Gull (27″)   4th February

Always to be seen flying over and quite often a visitor to the scraps.

Fieldfare

Rock Pipit

Glaucous Gull

Twite (5¼")   5th February

A pair, perhaps local breeding birds, visited the garden the day after we moved in.

Lapwing (12")   9th February

One of the first migrants, and birds were flying north on 9th February, a typical date.

Snipe (10½")   15th February

We have had Snipe in the garden on several occasions, even amongst the cabbages, but our first was seen flying up from the Boini Mire, south of the shop, where they nest.

Jack Snipe (7½")   15th February

One flew up from my feet as I began to rebuild the stone dykes around the back garden. One or two are about the shop most years, generally in the Boini Mire.

Golden Plover (11")   15th February

Another species we have seen all months of the year since our first in mid-February 1978.

Merlin (11 - 13")   21st February

Absolute panic among the garden birds — and there was our first Merlin dashing past in typical fashion. Sometimes Merlins come into the garden after prey.

Skylark (7")   24th February

A typical date for returning Skylarks. A regular garden bird from March to November and has nested.

Ringed Plover (7½")   24th February

Birds flying north, calling, at the end of February — another typical date.

Twite

Jack Snipe

Merlin

Curlew (22″)   25th February

Recorded all months of the year, the first were a flock flying north in late February.

Oystercatcher (17″)   26th February

Another late-February regular, when migration on the isle becomes quite noticeable.

Jackdaw (13″)   27th February

How nice it would be to have cliff-nesting Jackdaws as they have in Orkney. We have to make do with migrants, our first was a single bird on 27th February.

Stonechat (5″)   27th February

Just made it! A long standing Fair Isle game, to try and see a Stonechat before March. A few since, in spring and autumn.

Wood Pigeon (16″)   2nd March

May turn up on the isle at any time of year and our first bird looked a little lost as they do in such a barren place.

Gannet (36″)   5th March

Our first bird was flying north past the west cliffs, but an adult flew over the shop in August 1980.

Kestrel (13½″)   8th March

Recorded all months, but we had to wait until 8th March for our first.

Meadow Pipit (5¾″)   9th March

A typical date for returning birds. Has nested in the back garden.

Pink-footed Goose (24 - 30″)   9th March

Good numbers seen flying south most autumns but our first was a single bird in spring.

Stonechat

Kestrel

Meadow Pipit

Rook (18″)   20th March

One flying north on 20th March and several seen since, including one or two striding around the front garden.

Black-headed Gull (15″)   1st April

Probably the least common of the 'common' gulls on the isle, although recorded all months. Our first was a single adult flying north.

Common Gull (16″)   2nd April

A typical date for returning migrants although, again, recorded all months. Often visits the garden in search of scraps.

Lesser Black-backed Gull (21″)   2nd April

Our third 'new' gull in two days. We see them regularly between late March and October.

Reed Bunting (6″)   2nd April

Visits the garden most years on spring and autumn migration. Six together in October 1982, but our first was a single.

Great Grey Shrike (9½″)   2nd April

Sue saw our first while washing up! One or two of these striking birds have visited the garden most years in spring or autumn and a ringed Blackcap we had been feeding for 10 days in October 1982 finally fell prey to one. We awoke to find the Shrike devouring the Blackcap in the roses.

Pied Wagtail (7″)   3rd April

One of each sub-species — White and Pied — pecking around the back garden pond on 3rd April. Several of each seen since on migration.

Reed Bunting

Great Grey Shrike

Pied Wagtail

<u>Wheatear</u> (5¾″)   3rd April

One or two seen before the end of March most years, but our first in 1978 was early April. A pair nest in the front dyke every year, usually rearing two broods.

Chaffinch (6″)   3rd April

Probably the most surprising feature of migration we have seen at Stackhoull was the 95 male Chaffinches at the chicken corn in the front garden in April 1980. They somewhat overshadowed our first record — a single male — on 3rd April 1978.

Dunnock (5¼″)   3rd April

Dunnock visit the garden in spring and autumn most years and it may not be long before a pair attempt to nest in the roses.

Robin (5½″)   3rd April

The last of our 'new' birds on a memorable day! Seen regularly on migration and occasionally birds winter on the isle.

<u>Black Redstart</u> (5½″)   4th April

Several Black Redstarts have visited the garden since our first in 1978 and, as elsewhere, prefer the vicinity of stone walls and old buildings.

Mistle Thrush (10½″)   5th April

Never actually in the garden, but we have seen several, particularly on the Houll, since our first three in 1978.

Redshank (11″)   5th April

Seen most months in the fields around the shop, our first on 5th April.

Wheatear

Black Redstart

Ring Ouzel (9½")   5th April
Two males on the Houll on 5th April — a good spot for the species.
Odd birds have visited the garden but, at the first sign of humans,
are off.

Whooper Swan (60")   6th April
One of the three birds which arrived on the isle at the beginning of
April was seen flying north over the shop on 6th. Occasionally seen
in spring and regularly in autumn.

Brambling (5¾")   7th April
One of our favourites! Many have visited the garden in spring and
autumn since our first, a lovely male, in early April 1978.

Ruff (9 -11½")   15th April
A female Ruff (Reeve) spent much of the day in the ditch south of
the shop on 15th April, 1978 and we have seen several since, mostly
in the autumn, including two in the pond across the road in 1982.

Great Skua (23")   20th April
Our first 'Bonxie' as the bird is called locally flew North on 20th
April and we see them daily from late April - October. Whenever a
large bird of prey arrives during the summer, Bonxies mob them
relentlessly, often driving them off the isle.

Puffin (12")   20th April
Hardly a garden bird. Our only reasonably close sighting was of an
adult flying across the isle from west to east for some unknown
reason.

Ring Ouzel

Brambling

Great Skua

Goldcrest (3½") 23rd April

Surprisingly scarce as a garden bird, although one or two are seen annually in spring and autumn. As if their journeys weren't hazardous enough, these tiny birds are pecked at by our chickens if they ever come within range.

Tree Pipit (6") 29th April

A somewhat stronger looking bird than the Meadow Pipit, particularly in flight. Generally seen on the isle in small parties although our first garden bird was a single. Only recorded on migration in spring and autumn.

Greenfinch (5¾") 29th April

Rather uncommon on the isle and now probably seen less frequently than Rosefinch. Generally seen in two's and three's, and records are mainly late March -April (our first rather late — 29th), and late October - November.

Redstart (5½") 30th April

A regular visitor to the garden on migration, but often difficult to see because of the bird's retiring nature. The boat our children play on just outside the shop is a favourite perch for these lovely birds. Our first was a female.

Pied Flycatcher (5") 30th April

Seen in spring and autumn most years when we often set posts in the garden to attract them. Males, females and young birds have all used our look-out posts to swoop down for flies. In a particularly quiet spell in September 1979 a Pied Flycatcher just outside the garden brought birders running to see it, so few birds were there on the isle!

Goldcrest

Redstart

Pied Flycatcher

Whinchat (5")   30th April

Another regular visitor to the garden on migration. Very variable
plumage and, in September 1982, when several were in the vicinity,
the differences were strikingly evident. A beautiful bright male —
like a butterfly as it flew — was present in 1979, but our first was
somewhat duller.

Willow Warbler (4¼")   1st May

Recorded in spring and autumn each year since our first in 1978.
There may be up to six in the rose bushes at any one time — all
different — some yellower than others, some with dark legs. Once
or twice we have heard birds singing — a strange sound amid so
barren a landscape.

Wryneck (6½")   2nd May

It is a complete waste of time searching for Wrynecks on the isle:
they may be almost anywhere. More often than not they are flushed
quite accidentally, as nearly all those which have visited the garden
have been. The most obliging was on the grass directly below the
kitchen window one afternoon in September 1982. Sue and several
visitors saw it while having coffee in our kitchen 'tea-room'. I was
out! We had seen our first from bed on 2nd May, 1978.

Woodcock (13½")   4th May

Also likely to turn up anywhere on the isle. We have flushed them
from all parts of the garden and I caught one by hand in 1980.
Woodcock may be seen on the isle at any time of year when the
wind is south-east, but the largest numbers are seen in late
October/November. It is a sure sign at this time of year, that if
there are Blackbirds around the crofts, there are Woodcock on the
hill.

Whinchat

Wryneck

Woodcock

Arctic Skua (18″)   5th May

Returns to the isle towards the end of April, from which time until September, birds, often in pairs, are seen flying to and from their nest sites at the north end of the isle. A lovely pale bird flew over us on 5th May, 1978 — our first.

Hawfinch (7″)   5th May

Where else but Fair Isle could one get such views of a Hawfinch as we had of our first bird in 1978? This bird (and one in 1980) joined the local sparrows outside the kitchen window, eating the mixed corn we had put out for that specific purpose. Both birds spent much of their stay in the garden — ample reward for the cost of the corn!

Redpoll (5″)   6th May

More often heard flying over than seen in the garden, but many have paid us a visit, mainly in late autumn. Extremely variable in plumage, and we have seen the whole range of 'Lesser' and 'Mealy' types in spring and autumn.

Swallow (7½″)   7th May

A pair flew north on 7th May and birds have attempted to nest on the isle in recent years, on two or three occasions. Often seen flying around the house catching insects in the summer months.

Green Sandpiper (9″)   8th May

Not exactly a 'garden bird' and only just on our list. One seen flying over on 8th May, 1978.

Arctic Skua

Hawfinch

Redpoll

Collared Dove (11″)   9th May

Our first was almost 25 years after my own first sighting of the species in Norfolk when the bird was a relative newcomer to the British Isles.

Whitethroat (5½″)   9th May

Far more common in spring than autumn although we have seen them in the garden at both seasons. 9th May is a typical date for the first arrival.

Turtle Dove (11″)   11th May

Once they find the garden corn Turtle Doves keep coming back for more, as our first one did in May 1978.

Short-eared Owl (15″)   14th May

The first we saw flew slowly past the shop late one evening, since when we have flushed several from the back garden, particularly in the autumn.

Red-backed Shrike (6¾″)   19th May

The reasonably sheltered area directly south of the shop is a favourite area for Red-backed Shrikes in spring and autumn. The birds swoop down for insects from the fence posts and often work their way up to the garden. A pair visited the garden on 19th May, 1978 and our first glimpse was of the male looking down from an old dock — at a Wryneck.

House Martin (5″)   19th May

Well, they nest on Westray in Orkney, so if we get a hot enough summer, who knows? Birds are seen at odd times throughout the summer, often flying around the white-painted houses in search of insects.

Whitethroat

Short-eared Owl

Red-backed Shrike

Blackcap (5½″)   23rd May

A regular visitor to the garden on migration, often as late as the end of November. Many fall prey to Merlins and other birds of prey as a ringed female which had spent several days in the garden finally did — to a Great Grey Shrike.

Cuckoo (13″)   27th May

A brown (hepatic) bird spent much of the time around the shop on 27th May, 1978 and we have seen several others in the summer since, all the normal grey colour types.

Sparrowhawk (11 - 15″)   27th May

Our first bird soared slowly north over the shop. We see odd birds in spring and autumn most years, and occasionally, in winter. We have witnessed the demise of several unsuspecting sparrows, plucked from the roses by a raiding Sparrowhawk.

Spotted Flycatcher (5½″)   28th May

Another species which, having found the garden, will stay if left undisturbed, catching flies from around the white walls and amongst the rotting fruit we put out for that purpose. A typical spring date, and in autumn, most records are in September.

Swift (6½″)   29th May

Recorded annually in summer and although the first we saw was in May, by far the largest numbers are seen in July. Over 160 in July 1981 is the largest number on record for the isle.

Blackcap

Sparrowhawk

Spotted Flycatcher

Linnet (5¼″)   31st May

Quite uncommon on Fair Isle, we have only seen three or four in the garden since our first — a male in May 1978.

Chiffchaff (4¼″)   31st May

A few visit the garden most years on migration, particularly in autumn, when, as in October 1980, there may be birds of three different colour-types present at the same time, including the Siberian 'tristis' types.

Sand Martin (4¾″)   31st May

One flying north on 31st May and a few seen most years between April and October.

Hen Harrier (17 - 20″)   2nd June

Our first was a lovely adult male flying past the shop in early June. We have seen both males and females since and one bird in autumn 1982 came and hovered above the roses several times in search of prey.

Garden Warbler (5½″)   2nd June

Another species which is far more numerous in the autumn, when up to seven have been in the garden together. We have seen two individuals with several white feathers on their wings and mantle.

Bar-tailed Godwit (15″)   30th June

Odd birds seen flying over on migration, as our first was in June 1978.

Linnet

Hen Harrier

Garden Warbler

Peregrine (15 - 19″)   8th July

Although we have seen Peregrines every month of the year, they generally keep to the north end of the isle. We watched a pair displaying over Hoini in March 1979.

Greenshank (12″)   28th August

In answer to my whistles a lost migrant came down and almost landed in the garden in August 1978. A few others seen since on migration.

Black-headed Bunting (6½″)   31st August

A lovely bright male on the fence by the Kirk in 1978 could be easily identified even as far away as our garden. It looked wild so we ticked it!

Barnacle Goose (23 - 27″)   29th September

A flock flying south in 1978 were our first from the garden and we see flocks every autumn and occasionally in spring.

Bean Goose (28 - 35″)   29th September

One spent the day around the shop on 29th September, 1978, since when we have seen a few in autumn and winter.

Richard's Pipit (7″)   29th September

Our third new 'garden' bird on another memorable day. I flushed this first bird from the roadside as I went up for our milk. We have seen birds both in and around the garden most years and more than one bird on several occasions. One bird in 1980 spent over a week on the isle and for much of that time was to be seen in the long tussocky grass in our back garden.

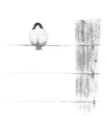

Black-headed Bunting

Richard's Pipit

Red-breasted Merganser (23″)   30th September

A pair flew south during a strong migration of thrushes in 1978.

Lapland Bunting (6″)
                                                     30th September

Although we have seen Lapland Buntings on many occasions in the fields around the shop, we have only once managed to entice the species into the garden. Birds in all plumages have been seen, including a few lovely bright males in spring.

Lesser Whitethroat (5¼″)   1st October

Such individual variation in plumage for so drab a species! One or two in the roses most years in spring and autumn.

Yellow-browed Warbler (4″)
                                                     1st October

Sue saw our first while I was playing golf at the South Lighthouse! I managed to see the same bird along the road the following day, but had to wait until October 1980 before my first garden bird, in the roses. We have seen four or five altogether, all in October.

Cormorant (36″)   6th October

Almost all our sightings of this species have been in October, when flocks can occasionally be seen flying south.

Greylag Goose (30 - 35″)   9th October

We have seen a few in spring but far more in the autumn, as our first flock was, flying south on a typical date.

Lapland Bunting

Yellow-browed Warbler

Ring-necked Duck (17″)   11th October
This bird was on the isle for a few days before it was finally identified on 9th October. We had seen it briefly on the 8th at Field, and on the 11th it flew south over the shop with a flock of Greylag Geese.

Grey Heron (36″)   2nd November
Herons drop into the Boini Mire from time to time, most records being in the last three months of the year.

Pochard (18″)   8th December
Very few records since we came to the isle. Our only record was a bird in the pond just across the road.

Mallard (23″)   23rd December
Quite surprising that we had to wait so long for our first Mallard. Seen all months since, often in pairs.

1979

Red Kite (24″)   15th January
Pure good fortune played a big part in adding this species to the island list. As I stepped out of the door to go for a walk the Kite was slowly drifting north being mobbed by the local crows. We stood outside and watched it flap slowly up the isle and out of sight, its lovely bright rusty-coloured tail and pale underwing patches making it most obvious, even from a great distance.

Yellowhammer (6½″)   18th January
One of the few migrants which, in the winter at least, does not look out of place on Fair Isle. One or two seen most years between October and April.

Ring-necked Duck

Red Kite

Yellowhammer

Buzzard (20 - 22″)   30th January

Quite a rarity on the isle and all our garden sightings were in early 1979 when we saw three individuals. The first was a particularly dark bird, the second somewhat paler, and the third was a pale bird typical of the North Scandinavian populations and very similar to. Rough-legged Buzzard.

Goldeneye (18″)   12th February

A single bird flew north past the shop in February 1979, our only sighting.

Shelduck (24″)   21st February

A pair in the field west of the shop on a typical date. Two birds a year is just about par for the isle.

Coot (15″)   24th February

A Coot spent a day waddling to and from the pond west of the shop in late February. It would run and hide in the stone dykes whenever disturbed.

Teal (14″)   9th March

Our first record was in 1979, a drake, and it had a quiet time compared to the drake which landed in the Boini Mire in 1982, and was relentlessly harrassed and pursued by the Houll domestic drake. A comical sight!

Grasshopper Warbler (5″)   12th May

A bird reeling in the long grass in the back garden was yet another strange sound we have heard on the isle. It was about for a few days and we could hear it from bed at night. A few seen since, all in autumn.

Buzzard

Shelduck

Grasshopper Warbler

Yellow Wagtail (6½")   15th May

We have seen several races of Yellow Wagtail around the shop since our first in May 1979. Very variable and I have seen more than one Yellow wagtail giving a 'Citrine' Wagtail call. Far more numerous in spring, but quite rare some years.

Bluethroat (5½")   23rd May

The bird we had been waiting for! Our disappointment at not seeing one in 1978 has been more than compensated for over the next four years. Our first, a male, spent the day in the front garden. We left it undisturbed, and when our two elder children came in from school we ushered them in through the store door so as they could look out through the shop window and see it. Their 'oooh's' and 'aaah's' said it all!

12th May, 1981, is without doubt the most outstanding day since we came to Fair Isle. Three males and a female Bluethroat were in the garden together, and two of the males spent a whole week singing and displaying, often right outside the kitchen window. The pile of rotting fruit we put out was a great attraction to them, and they took it in turns to feed in full view of our gaze.

Our only autumn visitor to the garden was a bird which spent the day at our compost heap on 3rd October, 1982.

Yellow Wagtail

Bluethroat

Arctic Tern (15″)   30th May

We see far more Arctic Terns than Common Terns flying over the shop, the longer streamers of the former being quite noticeable at a reasonable distance.

Hobby (12 - 14″)   1st June

A Hobby flew past us as we had dinner on the front lawn on 1st June, 1979. We had been watching a female Red-backed Shrike catching insects in the Boini Mire and, as we stood up to watch the Hobby, we saw it chasing the Shrike in and out of the fence wires before finally catching it. We later examined the pile of feathers left near the Kirk! One seen most years since, including a bird in 1982 which allowed approach to within ten yards.

Marsh Warbler (5″)   2nd June

If you want to see Marsh Warbler, come to Fair Isle for the first week of June! We have had a few in the garden, all in this period. The olive-green plumage is very different to the rusty-tinged brown of the Reed Warbler in spring, and where else could one get such views of both species?

Subalpine Warbler (4¾″)   1st June

Relegated to the bottom of the page, as the bird caught earlier at the hostel was released here at Stackhoull!

Hobby

Marsh Warbler

Subalpine Warbler

Sedge Warbler (5″)   6th June

Another annual visitor to the garden, and in most years seen in both spring and autumn. Our first bird was a tired migrant which found the first branch it came to and immediately went to sleep. The strip of corn we plant each year in the front garden is an attraction to the species, but it was really planted to attract the much rarer Aquatic Warbler!

Rustic Bunting (5¾″)   11th June

My personal favourite. The first we saw was a beautiful male on the fence just over the front wall. It was a foggy day but the bird sat there for several minutes before flying off. As is often the case with the species in spring, it was not seen again. It is also worth stating that the species shows no preference for a particular habitat in spring, and may turn up anywhere. I have seen birds on the top of Ward Hill, in the Boini Mire, and on stoney ground near the airstrip. Most autumn birds are, however, seen around the stubble-fields.

A female paid a brief visit to the garden in October 1980 — our only true 'garden' bird.

Sandwich Tern (16″)   12th July

Two birds flew north in fog on 12th July, our only sighting. Two or three birds a year is about average for the isle in spite of the large colonies in Orkney.

Sedge Warbler

Rustic Bunting

Crossbill (6½″)   25th July

Our daughter Hazel, who was eight at the time, came running indoors shouting 'there's a Crossbill on the chimney'. Before I could get outside we saw the bird fly down and into one of the cabbages we had left for seed. There, sure enough, was a Crossbill. It looked somewhat lost and only stayed in the garden for a minute or two. It was a green bird, probably a young female.

Common Tern(14″)   28th July

We occasionally see Common Terns flying over during midsummer, probably birds from the colony at the North Haven.

Spotted Redshank (12″)   21st August

Like Greenshank and Whimbrel, Spotted Redshank are easy to whistle down. This bird, our only one, almost landed on the shop roof in response to my calls.

Barred Warbler (6″)   23rd August

Rather a strange looking bird, the Barred Warbler. The birds somehow look unwell and of a rather sad disposition. All our garden records have been in August and September and, although I'm not given to predictions, I get the feeling that it will not be long before Fair Isle's first spring bird turns up.

These big clumsy warblers give away their presence in the roses, the tops of which can be seen swaying about under the bird's weight. The birds plumage is far less blue than most books show, although there is considerable individual variation.

Crossbill

Barred Warbler

Icterine Warbler (5¼")   9th September

What opportunities our roses have given us to study birds which, in other parts of Britain, would be hard enough to find. Icterine Warblers in particular take full advantage of them and two or three individuals have roosted in the more dense bushes. Our first 'garden' bird spent the whole of the day in the front garden, its pale wing panels most conspicuous as it worked its way among the foliage catching insects.

Another rather clumsy warbler, the swaying roses announcing the bird's presence. If only Lanceolated Warblers were so obliging!

Scarlet Rosefinch (5¾")   21st September

It must be bad enough being more drab than a sparrow, but these birds look stupid as well! (We have however, never seen an adult male). A regular visitor to the garden in spring and autumn since our first in September 1979. On one occasion, in spring 1981, we had two birds feeding together outside the kitchen window.

In spite of the drabness, the plumage can be quite variable, some birds, particularly in autumn, having quite pronounced wing-bars. One or two individuals (probably young males) have shown a pinky-buff wash around the tail and rump. The amount of streaking on the underparts is also quite variable.

The species often consorts with the local sparrows and, although they do not call all that often, the canary-like note is very distinct.

Icterine Warbler

Scarlet Rosefinch

Siskin (4¾″)   11th October
Our eldest son, Hayden, found our first Siskin, a male, in the back garden. Quite a regular garden visitor on migration but, infuriatingly, nearly always on dull, wet days.

Wigeon (18″)   14th October
Several Wigeon are seen flying over each year in spring and autumn, our first were on a typical date.

Long-eared Owl (14″)   30th October
I watched our first Long-eared Owl flying down the road in front of me as I returned from a walk. The bird went round the side of the house and out of sight. As I came round the corner of the building there was the bird, on the garden wall. There was no way I could get indoors for my camera!

Arctic Redpoll (5″)   29th December
This bird spent its two-day stay at North Shirva — so near yet so far. We could see its paleness from Stackhoull however, its pure white rump, double white wing-bar and white underparts making it very noticeable even at such a distance.

1980

Moorhen (13″)   30th March
Our first was in the Boini Mire in 1980, but a bird in October 1982 spent two days feeding in the garden with the local Starlings.

Eider (23″)   30th March
A female seen flying high over the west cliffs probably looking for a suitable nest-site.

Siskin

Long-eared Owl

Arctic Redpoll

Grey Wagtail (7″)   1st April

A male, ringed less than an hour earlier at the hostel, was in the ditch just outside the garden at lunchtime. It did not stay long, and as would be expected, most sightings of this species on the isle are towards the north end where the streams are generally faster flowing.

Razorbill (16″)   4th May

A deliberate attempt to tick this species. A lunch-time watch towards the west cliffs was enough.

Dunlin (7″)   11th May

None in yet, but one or two have come close. A few seen in spring and autumn most years.

Red-headed Bunting (6″)   18th May

Although birds of this species are always suspected of being 'escapes', this individual was in perfect condition and made every effort to be accepted as a wild bird. It visited the garden on two or three occasions but flew off at the slightest disturbance. This bird would probably have had to fly only half the distance the Yellow-browed Bunting of 1980 had to reach Fair Isle.

Snowy Owl (22 - 26″)   21st May

Having missed a female at Lower Stoneybrake (our next-door neighbour) in 1979, we thought our chance of adding this species to our garden list had gone, but as I went out for a walk one evening, the cries of terns made me look round. There, flapping slowly down the isle and right over the shop was the Snowy Owl seen earlier in the day near the airstrip. The bird carried on down the isle and left in a Southerly direction.

Grey Wagtail

Red-headed Bunting

Snowy Owl

Wood Warbler (5″)   3rd September

This lovely bold-looking warbler is quite uncommon on the isle. We could see our first on one of the fence-wires on the Houll. What was probably the same bird came into the garden shortly afterwards and spent its time catching insects in the roses. The bright green upperparts, yellow throat and upperbreast and white belly make this a very striking bird.

Another of my personal favourites. Oh for a singing male one year!

Reed Warbler (5″)   9th September

A surprisingly long wait — over a year since our first Marsh Warbler — for this species and we have still only seen this one in the garden. The rusty tinge to the plumage is very noticeable on the isle.

Buff-breasted Sandpiper (8″)   18th September

I twice saw this American wader flying over the shop. On the first occasion it flew down the isle from Upper Stoneybrake and I watched it heading towards Meoness where it was later identified. On the second occasion it again flew south, later the same day, in company with Ringed Plovers. In flight the white underwing and general paleness were most noticeable, as were the long pointed wings. All the records of this species on Fair Isle have been in September, four of the six between the 17th and 21st.

Wood Warbler

Reed Warbler

Buff-breasted Sandpiper

Hoopoe (11″)   8th October

A familiar ring about the occurence of this bird in the garden — I was looking for it in the field to the east of the shop! Sue saw it clinging to the wall outside the kitchen window, but it soon flew off and spent the rest of the day around the rocks just outside the garden. Notoriously difficult to locate on the isle unless they fly, the pinkish plumage blending in with the colour of the dead grass. Our only sighting.

White-fronted Goose (26 - 30″)   11th October

One sighting only, a single bird flying south with Greylags.

Wren (3¾″)   24th October

The island Wrens keep very much to the beaches and are seldom seen inland. However, a few may be seen around the crofts in late autumn and winter. It seems strange with all the excellent nest-sites on the isle, particularly in the stone walls, that this species should nest exclusively around the shoreline.

Short-toed Lark (5½″)   5th November

I heard this bird flying towards me as I worked in the back garden preparing the children's bonfire. It flew over the house and I dashed round to tell Sue. To my amazement it had dropped into the front garden and, although I had time to identify it even without binoculars, I was too close and the bird flew off. What was probably the same bird was seen at Field a day or so later.

Hoopoe

Wren

Short-toed Lark

Bullfinch (6¼")   7th November

What lovelier bird than the big Northern Bullfinch? And what a shame they are generally recorded in November when the light is so poor! Our first two, a pair, were on the washing line in the back garden and spent much of their stay flitting in their own quiet way between the shop and the post office. Their plaintive call is easy to mimic and on several occasions I have called Bullfinches to us when they have been in the vicinity.

Water Rail (11")   17th November

If ever a bird deserved 'E' for effort it is the Water Rail! Every year a few try to winter on the isle and many of these are found dead or dying in hard weather. Our first garden visitor in 1980 spent much of its stay around our chicken run and would run into the nest-boxes for cover. Another bird, in 1981, spent its time in the front garden and would run and hide in the stone walls if disturbed.

1981

Iceland Gull (24")   15th March

Until 1983 our only sighting was a bird flying over in March 1981, when one or two had been seen at the South Harbour for some time. A quite unprecedented influx took place at the end of 1982, when I saw up to 12 together in the same area. Three adults were found dead and birds were often to be seen walking around the fields searching for grubs in association with Herring Gulls. We saw several about the shop early in 1983, on one occasion three together.

Bullfinch

Water Rail

Iceland Gull

Sandhill Crane (40″)   26th April

Well, the illustration is what we saw, a huge silhouette flying up
and down the isle. The bird was between us and the sun each time
we saw it, but even so the bird did appear to have a suggestion of
Common Crane about the head and neck and it may well be worth
having a careful look at any future lone Cranes.

Wood Sandpiper (8″)   12th May

Our one and only Wood Sandpiper spent much of the day in the
Boini Mire, but early in the evening, much to our amazement, it
flew past the kitchen window and landed next to a tiny puddle in
our top vegetable plot. It stayed in the garden for over half an hour
and looked most odd pecking about alongside the Starlings. Hardly
a garden bird — but this is Fair Isle!

Tree Sparrow (5½″)   16th May

About time too! Although recorded annually on the isle we had to
wait a long time for our first garden visitor. Tree Sparrows have
nested on the isle sporadically and odd birds have hybridised with
House Sparrows producing some rather strange offspring. In some
ways we were disappointed to tick this species as there was
something quaint about a garden list with no Tree Sparrow.

Sandhill Crane

Wood Sandpiper

Tree Sparrow

Corncrake (10½")   4th June

Sue and I were watching our son Kevin playing in the front garden, when he suddenly jumped back and a startled Corncrake flew out from almost under his feet. Kevin came running indoors looking a little worried, so we told him that the bird he had just seen was a Corncrake. 'That cornflake frightened me', he said in typical three-year-old fashion!

Alpine Swift (10")   5th June

This bird really was a bonus. We had missed one in April — we were away on holiday — and the likelihood of another on Fair Isle in the same year seemed rather remote. We saw this second bird with common Swifts soaring over the isle on 5th June, but we almost missed it as well. The bird had flown north, right past the shop the previous day and the foreign visitor who had been the only person to see it did not realise that the species was so rare in Britain, and only mentioned his sighting casually over lunch. Fortunately for us all it was relocated again, quite accidentally, near the North Light, and spent several days about the isle.

Black Guillemot (13½")   10th June

As I stood looking for Common Guillemots in an effort to add it to the garden list, a Black Guillemot flew from one of the ledges in North Reeva, where the species nests.

Guillemot (16½")   10th June

This species quickly followed the last onto our garden list and we have seen one or two flying across the isle since.

Corncrake

Alpine Swift

Honey Buzzard (20 - 23″)   10th July

If only all the other large birds of prey which visit the isle would follow this bird's example. It kept away from the cliffs and thereby avoided the fate which befalls so many raptors which arrive here — Fulmar-oiling. For several days this handsome bird could be seen striding about the grassy fields, searching for wasps. On fine days it would soar up above the fields until driven back to earth by the Skuas.

Another bird we saw briefly in 1982 was less fortunate and was found dead, covered in Fulmar oil.

Grey Plover (11″)   15th September

I had heard one or two previously, before finally seeing what on Fair Isle is a surprisingly scarce migrant. Very few seen since.

Pallas's Reed Bunting (5¾″)   17th September

Britain's second, was just outside the garden briefly the day it was found. This bird, a first-year, was quite streaked and, although it did look a little different, was very similar to Reed Bunting and has probably been overlooked previously. The moustachial stripes did not reach the bill, the bird was slightly smaller than Reed Bunting and the lesser coverts were greyish, but I would hesitate to try and identify the species in the field. Fortunately this bird was quickly caught and the identification confirmed.

Honey Buzzard

Pallas's Reed Bunting

Great Snipe (11″)   22nd September

Jimmy Wilson of Schoolton discovered this bird early one morning and alerted the observatory. I was particularly interested in seeing the bird as I had seen what I felt sure was a Great Snipe in September 1978, and so went across with the first birders to arrive on the scene. It didn't take us long to find the bird — exactly where Jimmy had said. My suspicions were confirmed, the Woodcock-like shape being quite diagnostic. The white in the tail was only noticeable at close range on this first-year bird, but the bold white markings on the wings were very distinct even at a fair distance.

The bird spent several days around the shop and we saw it on many occasions.

Roller (12″)   22nd September

Our most exciting and unexpected bird — again a complete fluke. I had gone to the rear of the shop to look for a small Bunting which had just flown over the roof, when I noticed what I thought was a displaced stone on one of the walls. It was the Roller and once again shows what a big part luck plays in birding. A new bird for the isle, and it didn't take us long to alert other birders on the isle, who came running from all directions not knowing what the bird was. Some had been looking for the Great Snipe, others for a Yellow-breasted Bunting and a third group were trying to catch a Short-toed Lark. In a very short time there were over thirty birders in the back garden enjoying superb views of the Roller, which after about forty minutes flew up and over us as if to show us its bright blue underwings. Unfortunately the bird was found long-dead under a haystack the following spring.

Great Snipe

Roller

Isabelline Shrike (7″)   12th October

This shrike, found on 9th October at Midway, finally came close enough for us to put it on our garden list on 12th. A very striking bird and quite different from any of the many Red-backed Shrikes we have seen. The black through the eye contrasted starkly with the pale sandy-grey colouration of the upperparts and the pinky-buff of the underparts. The rusty-red tail too was very conspicuous and long-looking and the white patch at the base of the primaries very noticeable. The tail had a dark subterminal bar, about half an inch long.

At least one Blackcap and a Goldcrest fell prey to the bird during its stay on the isle. One year later and one wonders how many Pallas's Warblers it would have eaten.

Waxwing (7″)   31st October

If only these birds had known that I had thrown out some cranberries earlier in the day, we might have been able to keep them on the isle a little longer, but as is usual with the species the birds stayed for a very short time. We could see them on the TV aerial at North Shirva and that was as close as they got.

The birds were of course very tame and we did not hesitate in taking the children down to see them. The two we had seen initially joined two others on the washing-line at Midway. Oh for a few rowan trees on the isle!

Isabelline Shrike

Waxwing

1982

Marsh Harrier (19 - 22″)   4th May

Although I had seen a Marsh Harrier briefly on 12th May, 1978, our first really good look at one was not until 1982. As usual with large birds of prey it had to run the gauntlet with the local skuas — as if the Fulmars weren't enough to contend with. We saw this bird soaring over the shop on many occasions, its lovely dark chocolate-brown plumage making a welcome contrast to the many white-bodied gulls which are a permanent feature of the Fair Isle sky. Once or twice we saw it perched on fence-posts, when its pale forehead was most conspicuous.

Goosander (26″)   7th May

It was a real surprise to see two male Goosanders flying down the isle one morning, although 1982 was a good year for the species on Fair Isle.

Ortolan Bunting (6½″)   16th May

The elusive Ortolan. One of the most difficult birds to locate on the isle as they may turn up in almost any habitat, and even in spring the birds are hard to spot on the ground. Two birds flew past me on 16th May and one was on the wall at Lower Stoneybrake the same day. The call is often the only indication of the bird's presence, being a loud version of the first note of the Chiffchaff's song and very like the 'tsip' note Starlings occasionally make. We heard birds flying over several times in May 1982 but as yet none have visited the garden — as far as we know.

Marsh Harrier

Ortolan Bunting

Bee-eater (11″)   5th June

This beautiful bird was discovered at Furse, north of the Observatory, before breakfast on 4th June (my birthday, and it is amazing how often rare birds turn up on that date!). A subsequent search for the bird turned up a Golden Oriole in the same spot. I joined a later search party but we gave up and wandered slowly back down the isle. A short time later we got word that the bird had been found below the post office. We had to wait until the following day to add it to the garden list and although we had excellent views of it elsewhere on the isle we were a little disappointed that it got no closer than 100 yards from the shop.

Quail (7″)   5th June

Although we had heard Quail calling in previous years we did not see one until 1982 when one was flushed in the field west of the shop. I was just on my way to dump some rubbish when the bird got up from under my feet. The bird was most obliging for a Quail and several observers obtained good views of it on the ground.

My only other sighting of the species was in 1960 back in my home-town of Gillingham where I had managed to stalk a calling male.

The birds are surprisingly pale in flight.

Knot (10″)   31st August

A beautiful adult Knot still with much of its summer plumage was with a flock of Turnstones just west of the shop on the 31st August. It looked a little out of place in the long grass.

Bee-eater

Quail

Sanderling (8")   9th September

There were several inland sightings of Sanderling on the isle in 1982, and after seeing one or two elsewhere, one finally flew over me in the garden on 9th September.

Great-spotted Woodpecker (9")   7th October

I had always wanted to see this species on the isle and having missed a few previously for one reason or other I dashed off down the isle to see this one. I needn't have bothered, as the following day it was working its way round the fence-posts near the shop. The bird looked huge on the isle, reminding one of just how different scale is here. It was quite confiding and allowed approach to within a few yards. I last saw the bird at the base of the west cliffs, still desperately searching for food.

Little Bunting (5¼")   11th October

At last! This species has cost us a small fortune in corn, which we would scatter around the garden every autumn in an effort to attract one in. We were beginning to think we would never succeed when suddenly on 12th October, there on the garden wall stood a real cracker. It flew down and joined the local sparrows at the corn, its bright rusty-coloured ear-coverts most prominent. We saw it several times that day, uttering the Robin-like 'tic' each time it flew — and I have yet to see a Little Bunting which did not call every time it took to the wing. Well worth waiting for, 15 or 16 years since I first saw one on Fair Isle, near Springfield.

Great-spotted Woodpecker

Little Bunting

Rough-legged Buzzard (20 - 24″)   13th October

A quite deliberate attempt to tick this species. Two birds turned up on the isle a day or two earlier and spent several weeks here reducing the local rabbit population considerably, the corpses of which could be seen in many places. I decided to stand outside at lunchtime just to see if I could see one above Ward Hill. To my surprise a few minutes later not only did I see one, but as if the bird seemed to know we wanted a closer look, it slowly drifted south and passed a few feet over our heads in the front garden.

Olive-backed Pipit (5¾″)   13th October

I had just been watching our first Rough-legged Buzzard when a large 'quiet' Thrush flew over me heading west (a Black-throated Thrush was found later that day). I decided to go and have a look for the bird but took only two steps into the field west of the shop when up from almost under my feet flew an Olive-backed Pipit. The bird called and landed no more than twenty feet away. The lovely olive-green colour of the back and the distinct head pattern were most conspicuous in the bright sunlight. The bird flew across the road and spent the afternoon striding about the back garden.

One can hardly be superstitious after a 13th as good as that!

Great Northern Diver (27 - 32″)   30th October

A typical date — most records of the species on the isle are in October and again just a case of looking up at the right time. The bird, our only record, was flying south towards the South Harbour where one had been seen earlier that day.

Rough-legged Buzzard

Olive-backed Pipit

Gyrfalcon (20 - 22")   9th December

If I could have chosen a species to finish on, this would have been the one.

A bird we had often hoped to see and once again found in rather fortuitous circumstances. I had gone for a walk for the first time in several days and, although I could tell by the behaviour of the local starlings that there was a bird of prey about, I was hardly expecting the sight that greeted me as I approached Kennaby. There, flying from the ruins, was a pure white bird with a longish tail, looking at first sight like a huge white Collared Dove. The bird disappeared briefly but was soon back on the wall at Kennaby, and I could now see just how white it was, with very few black spots.

This beautiful falcon spent the afternoon on the isle but was not seen the following day, when many of the islanders were looking out for it, in the hope of catching a glimpse of what, even on Fair Isle, is a very rare species.

Twice it flew right over us in the garden, no more than twenty feet from the ground, giving us the sort of views of a bird of prey one dreams about and its slow, languid flight meant that on each occasion we had ample time to study its features.

A grey bird of the Scandinavian race flew past me just outside the shop on 24th December. The tail on this bird did not appear as long as the white bird's, but the wings appeared even more rounded, and it was certainly much bigger and bulkier than any of the many Peregrines I have seen.

Gyrfalcon

THE KIRK

CHAPEL, MUSEUM and TAFT (unoccupied)

Part II

Birds seen elsewhere on the isle,
including most of the
Fair Isle 'specials'.

An aid to identification.

Pallas's Warbler (3¼")

1982 will go down as 'the year of the Pallas's Warbler'. With only three previous records of single birds (most previous records in Britain were on the east and south-east coasts) Fair Isle could hardly have been expected to be the venue for over ten in one day. How many were missed one can only guess, but allowing for the dearth of coverage of the west cliffs, it is quite probable that the total could well have been doubled. Most of the sightings were on the grassy slopes of the west cliffs, but birds were seen close to many of the crofts, although much to our chagrin, not one managed to find our garden.

This tiny warbler is smaller than a Goldcrest and just as confiding. One flew through my legs as I stood watching it, and other observers had similar incidents to relate. It is difficult to imagine so small a bird flying across the North Sea and just how many perish in the waters after failing to find land is pure conjecture. This bird is without doubt a wind-borne migrant to Fair Isle. All island records have been in October.

The plumage is most striking and quite different to any of the other warblers seen in Britain, the bright rump being the most prominent feature, noticeable from a considerable distance. The head seems disproportionately large and, when the bird is in certain attitudes, appears almost as big as the body.

It looks as if the chance of adding this species to our garden list has gone and it must remain for now 'the one that got away'.

Pallas's Warbler

Greenish Warbler (4¼")   16th September

A new species for me and I was glad to catch up with one at last so I could see just how the bird compared to the Siberian Chiffchaffs we see every autumn.

I had just looked at one particular spot on the isle and within five minutes was called back there to see my first Greenish Warbler. A familiar story on Fair Isle.

The bird was with two or three Willow Warblers from which it could be distinguished by its slighter shape and smaller size and its very white underparts. The legs, like some Willow Warblers, were dark brown.

Compared to the Siberian *tristis* Chiffchaffs the bird was greener and the whitish wing-bar and supercilium more distinct than in that species.

It has long been suspected that many of the records of Greenish Warbler in Great Britain were wrongly identified *'tristis'* Chiffchaffs and I hope that the plate opposite will help to clarify the differences. My own feelings are that it may be best to concentrate on leg colour as the black legs of Chiffchaffs are always distinct.

Arctic Warbler is a much stronger looking bird with heavier bill and pale legs.

One bird a year seems to be the recent Fair Isle average and with about twenty crofts on the isle we may have a while to wait before it is our turn for a 'garden' Greenish Warbler. The nearest so far was at Quoy.

Greenish Warbler

Chiffchaff

Arctic Warbler (4¾")

Another species which has so far avoided our garden and one we would like to see. One obstinate individual spent some time at North Shirva in 1980 but ventured no nearer than that. I suppose a 60x telescope from the roof would have put it on our list, but we may well have been accused of desperation tactics. A bird almost as close was at the east end of the Houll in 1978, but that too kept its distance.

A much stronger-looking bird than most other small phylloscopus recorded in Britain and this is a very useful feature. The wings are rather long and the bill large and dagger-like which probably helps to give the bird its strong appearance. Rounded wings tend to give warblers in general a 'weak' appearance. The most outstanding feature, however, is the striking supercilium which often appears to cut off the top of the bird's head. This feature is more noticeable at a distance when the birds can look very dark with a striking white line from the bill to the nape.

The upperparts are darker than Greenish and Willow Warblers, but are variable, some appearing greyer than the bird illustrated. The crown is darker than the rest of the upperparts.

The legs of all the individuals I have seen have been pale brown, similar to Willow Warblers.

Oh to see one of these beauties in the roses!

Arctic Warbler

Melodious Warbler (5")

Having just missed two Melodious Warblers previously on the isle I finally caught up with one in the plantation one lunchtime.

An American visitor who was about to leave on the plane alerted me to the bird, which he had seen very briefly, but which he was sure was not an Icterine Warbler. The bird had been in the Gully near one of the traps, but by the time I had walked north it had reached the plantation. I saw it from over 100 yards and its short rounded wings were immediately noticeable, giving it the appearance of a green and yellow Reed Warbler. The bird dived into the canopy of the plantation and I dashed off to the Observatory to alert the staff. On returning to the plantation we made a search of the area and drove the trap, but there was no sign of the bird. I was sure that no-one had been in the area and so we continued the search. We finally gave up after some twenty minutes or so, resigned to the fact that it was another near miss. As I walked off towards Setter I suddenly remembered the small roadside trap called 'North Grind', and there it was in the catching box — a Melodious Warbler.

Some can be very difficult to identify, but this bird had the typical short wings and faint pale wing-panel of the species, the former being the most reliable feature when separating the species from Icterine Warbler.

Melodious Warbler

Aquatic Warbler (5″)

Disappointingly scarce since we came to Fair Isle. Even more disappointing is the fact that we chose the years 1980, '81 and '82 to plant a patch of corn in the garden with the sole purpose of attracting this species and Yellow-breasted Bunting to it. Not one was seen on the isle during those years.

It seems to be a mid-August bird only and unless the wind is south-east between 5th and 20th none are recorded.

What opportunities one gets on Fair Isle! My first sighting of this species was in 1979 just east of the Kirk and to obtain such views as I had of so rare a bird is remarkable and makes one realise just how different birding is here when compared to mainland Britain, where species such as this will give only the briefest views.

In such a sparsely vegetated place the general colour of species such as Aquatic Warbler is most evident and immediately distinct. The pale sandy colour, much lighter than Sedge Warbler, distinguishes this species at once and my first view of an Aquatic Warbler flying away from me left me in no doubt as to what the species was.

So, if Aquatic Warbler is on your 'shopping list' come to Fair Isle in mid-August, hope for south-east winds and, if you should see one, try and flush it in our direction!

Savi's Warbler (5½″)

Just on my island list, as the bird present at the Observatory in 1981 flew out of the garden as I went past on the coal lorry. Warmer and rustier-looking than Reed Warbler.

Aquatic Warbler

Savi's Warbler

Pallas's Grasshopper Warbler (5¼")

If only birds such as this would turn up on the isle in better weather conditions. It is almost invariably south-east wind and infuriating drizzle when the rarest birds are found.

However, this bird was most obliging once it had been located. It trapped itself on the outside of one of the Heligoland traps and was quickly secured and then, after release in the hostel garden, gave everyone excellent views as it crept about beneath the rose bushes there.

Certainly the most striking feature in the field was the rusty rump, although this was far less evident in the hand. The pale grey 'shawl' around the nape was also very prominent, but the pale tips to the tail were disappointingly inconspicuous.

Although the measurements were only slightly larger than Grasshopper Warbler, the bird was far more bulky looking, with a deep belly, a feature reflected in the weight of the bird compared to that species.

Allowing for the polarisation of light which has the effect of intensifying certain differences in colour, it is quite probable that this species is in fact easier to identify at a distance, if observers concentrate on the colour of the rump rather than the tail-feathers.

The supercilium was less striking a feature than is generally stressed.

Pallas's Grasshopper Warbler

Lanceolated Warbler (4½")

In Britain, this bird is almost exclusively Fair Isle's property. All but two of the records have been here, mainly in late September.

Having said that, it is absolutely pointless coming to Fair Isle to look for one; you just book your holiday and hope that someone comes across one while you are here. I well remember searching the ditches in the late 60's hoping to find one. Roy Dennis, who was warden for several years in the 60's, never did see one on Fair Isle despite much diligent searching.

The species has become almost annual in the autumn since the mid-70's but most birds have been found fortuitously, so skulking are they. I have seen several and have watched many vain attempts by birdwatchers to flush them from small tussocks into which the birds had disappeared.

One would expect the species to turn up in the wet ditches, but records are from all parts of the isle including the heather and bracken at the north end.

Field descriptions are hardly useful for such a secretive bird but the species is like a diminutive Grasshopper Warbler and equally variable in colouration. I have illustrated two of the birds I have seen, one a very grey individual, the other quite rusty in general tone.

We may have almost trodden on several in the garden and not known a thing about it!

Lanceolated Warbler

River Warbler (5″)

A quite distinct species when seen well, the greenish upperparts being unstreaked and different from others of the genus. The gorget of streaks on the upper breast is variable and may be almost absent. Unfortunately the under tail-coverts are the most striking feature of the bird but one can hardly expect good views of them, as the bird is like all those of its family, very skulking. One very obliging bird in September, 1982, spent most of one day in the Observatory trap after release, but the individual of May, 1981, was unfortunately found dead at the North Haven the day after it was first seen.

Three records in the 16 months between May, 1981 and September, 1982, is remarkable and a friend who stayed with us in September, 1982, saw two River and three Lanceolated Warblers during his three-week stay and not one Blackbird!

That is Fair Isle!

Great Reed Warbler (7½″)

My only sighting was in 1978 when one of these huge unmistakeable warblers spent a few days on the isle. Like a giant Reed Warbler with a pale supercilium and twice as noisy. On arrival it took up territory on the isle, and could be heard singing from a considerable distance.

River Warbler

Great Reed Warbler

Yellow-browed Bunting (5½")

A new bird for the British list. The arrival of this bird at about the same time as the first Pine Bunting of 1980 and the Brünnich's Guillemot, almost lead to the biggest 'twitch' of all time. A group of birdwatchers on the Scilly Isles had a plane standing by to bring them direct to Fair Isle, but unfortunately the weather here was too bad for the plane to land and the trip had to be cancelled. Several birders did however travel all the way from the Scillies by conventional means and saw this bird at least (most also saw the Pine Bunting), and it is interesting to note that the cost of the trip was only slightly cheaper than the share of the charter would have been — and the latter would have saved four days travel time!

The Yellow-browed Bunting was certainly most obliging and allowed approach to within a few yards, spending almost the whole of its 12 day stay in one very small area. The bird looked more like an American sparrow than a bunting, its brightly coloured head contrasting starkly with its very drab body. Two pale wing-bars were the only noticeable feature apart from the head, the crown feathers of which were constantly kept raised. No doubt the next one will be completely different.

There was a certain resemblance to Little Bunting, although the bird was slightly bigger and bulkier looking. The call was half-way between Little and Rustic buntings and I write them down thus:

         Little . . . .   tic
         Y-browed . . . . . .   tsic
         Rustic . . . .   twic

It's on someone's garden list — but not ours!

Yellow-browed Bunting

Yellow-breasted Bunting (5½")

Probably the most predictable of the rare species which visit the isle, both in the timing of its arrival and its choice of habitat. Almost without exception (although still extremely rare, two to four individuals a year being the recent average) the species arrives in September and will only be found in the fields of standing corn. I believe that birds found elsewhere on the isle have either just arrived, or have just been flushed from one of the corn-fields. Once the corn has been cut the birds soon depart, preferring not to feed on the stubble along with the other species of bunting.

In spite of its habit of keeping to the standing corn, the bird is not difficult to locate, often announcing its presence with the quiet but distinct 'tsic' call and it really is a waste of time trying to flush the species as the birds will often sit tight when disturbed. If Yellow-breasted Bunting is on your shopping list, come to Fair Isle in September, select one of the fields of corn and sit and watch for it — while praying for south-east winds!

A smaller, dumpier bird than the Yellowhammer and, although as with most species of bunting the plumage is somewhat variable, the bird illustrated opposite is typical of those seen here.

Yellow-breasted Bunting

Pine Bunting (6½")

Although this bird resembled a Yellowhammer, there was no trace of yellow in the plumage and, particularly in flight, the general 'whiteness' was most noticeable. The bird often gave a hard 'twick' note, but I never heard it utter the longer 'trrrrp' call often used by Yellowhammers.

According to some authorities this species hybridises with Yellowhammer in Russia and this, coupled with the fact that some illustrators show first-year Yellowhammers in the same plumage as the bird illustrated, must leave some doubt as to the exact origins of this individual. I have certainly never seen a Yellowhammer approaching this bird in whiteness however.

Many Yellowhammers were present on the isle in the late autumn, 1980, and a male Pine Bunting was caught early in November, but unfortunately I did not see that bird.

Pine Bunting

Cretzschmar's Bunting (6¼″)

Hardly a description needed for this real beauty! The bird's head was a lovely soft bluey-grey and from a distance looked very much like the head of a Bearded Tit. Apart from the head the bird looked very much like an Ortolan, rather long, although the head itself looked somewhat bulbous.

It is perhaps worth noting that the chin and moustachial stripes were yellowish and not orange as is usually shown in most bird guides.

The second record for Britain, arriving just one day earlier than the previous bird, also a male, which was seen from 10th to 20th June, 1967.

Ortolan Bunting (6½″)

What a fine sight it must have been in past years, when this species was far more abundant in the spring, to see Ortolans on each croft during migration. Sadly the bird is now much rarer, very few being seen in spring or autumn, although the autumn birds tend to stay for a few days and in spite of their drab colour are generally easier to see. Even with such drab plumage it is amazing just how variable the species can be, the bird illustrated being typical of those seen in the autumn.

Cretzschmar's Bunting

Ortolan Bunting

Rustic Bunting (5¾″)

To me the most striking feature of this species is the rather spiteful look the birds have. Every one of the many I have seen on the isle has shown this feature prominently and it is probably formed by a combination of the bill shape and head pattern.

The bird illustrated is an autumn male, very similar to females and young birds, all showing the two prominent pale wing bars. The two pale, long parallel patches, one above and one below the ear coverts, are also very prominent at all ages.

A bird similar to the one illustrated paid a brief visit to the garden in October, 1980.

Black-headed Bunting (6½″)

I was particularly pleased to see the bird illustrated, in autumn 1982, having had frustratingly brief views of another female on Fair Isle in 1974. Although I have not seen a female Red-headed Bunting, I have seen two males and there is no doubt that Black-headed is a longer-looking bird, Red-headed appearing short and dumpy in comparison. It is probably pure coincidence that the 1974 female frequented the area near the Kirk, where a male was present in 1978.

Rustic Bunting

Black-headed Bunting

Some examples of the fifteen species of
bunting I have seen on the isle.

1.	Pine Bunting	October 1980
2.	Yellowhammer	October 1980
3.	Yellowhammer	October 1980
4.	Yellow-breasted Bunting	September 1977
5.	Rustic Bunting	October 1980
6.	Rustic Bunting	June 1979
7.	Little Bunting	October 1982
8.	Yellow-browed Bunting	October 1980
9.	Reed Bunting	April 1978
10.	Reed Bunting	October 1977
11.	Pallas's Reed Bunting	September 1981
12.	Corn Bunting	January 1978
13.	Ortolan Bunting	May 1978
14.	Ortolan Bunting	October 1979
15.	Cretzschmar's Bunting	June 1979
16.	Red-headed Bunting	May 1980
17.	Black-headed Bunting	September 1982
18.	Black-headed Bunting	August 1978
19.	Lapland Bunting	May 1978
20.	Lapland Bunting	October 1978
21.	Snow Bunting	February 1978
22.	Snow Bunting	June 1978

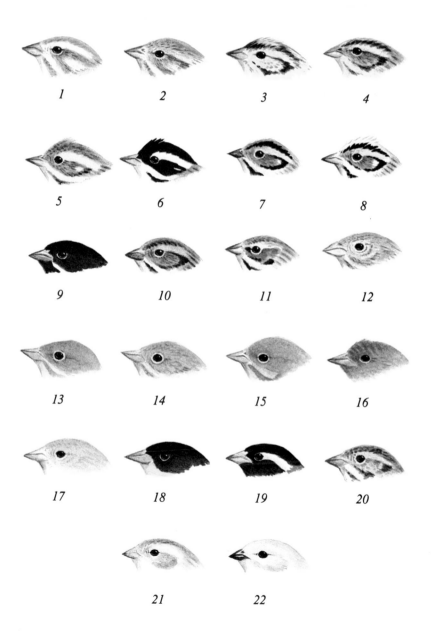

1 2 3 4

5 6 7 8

9 10 11 12

13 14 15 16

17 18 19 20

21 22

Song Sparrow (6″)

Rather Dunnock-like in its behaviour, this species joined up with one of the local flocks of House Sparrows and spent practically the whole of its three week stay on the isle shuffling around on the ground in search of corn.

The head was quite distinctly patterned, but by far the most outstanding field-mark was the dark diamond shape in the centre of the breast.

White-throated Sparrow (7″)

This bird had the tired, rather pop-eyed look of a long-distance runner who has just completed his first marathon. It had quite probably just completed the bird's equivalent — flying the North Atlantic.

As with most of the American sparrows, the head was the most striking feature, but the longish tail too was very noticeable.

Song Sparrow

White-throated Sparrow

Thrush Nightingale (6½")

A real Fair Isle special. Unfortunately there has only been one record since we came to live on Fair Isle, but the bird certainly made up for lack of numbers by resting and preening in the open in full view of the many observers who went to see it.

Hardly a beautiful species, but the bird certainly has a charm of its own, the sombre earth-brown tones, speckled breast, and slight rusty tail and upper tail-coverts giving the bird a rather tweedy look.

The rusty tinge is far less noticeable than in the Nightingale, and I have illustrated a female Redstart, a Nightingale and a Thrush Nightingale together to show the differences in bright sunlight, Nightingale appearing half-way between the other two species in general colouration of the tail and upper tail-coverts.

A red-letter bird, and still missing from one or two well-known birders' lists!

Thrush Nightingale

Redstart   *Nightingale*   *Thrush Nightingale*

Red-flanked Bluetail (5½")

Sad to say this bird was never anywhere near our garden and having been found near the Chapel and seen until dusk that day near Springfield, it was discovered at the North Haven the following morning. A very interesting point and surely a caution to consider more carefully the numbers of common species on the isle. A Redpoll at the north end of the isle may well be seen at the south end later in the day.

This bird really was a beauty and very obliging too. It spent most of its first day on the isle on a pile of cut turf, from which it would fly down to catch insects. In shape it more resembled Robin than Redstart, being rather large-headed and dumpy looking. No description is necessary regarding the plumage, but as with Bluethroat the blue did not show up well from a distance.

A delighted group of birders chartered a plane the day after the bird's discovery, walked down to the North Haven, saw the bird well, walked back to the plane and left the isle 50 minutes after arriving. One of the party, an elderly gentleman, had been to Shetland over a dozen times, but had never before visited Fair Isle. I'm sure they all felt the trip well worthwhile!

Red-flanked Bluetail

Bluethroat (5½")

I have included a plate of Bluethroats in this section although the species is illustrated in Part I.

I have found this species to be far less skulking than one is led to believe in most of the literature and, particularly in spring, the males are every bit as demonstrative and confiding as the Robin. Because of the blue throat one tends to expect that the birds will be easy to spot at considerable distance, but as is often the case in nature, the blue appears merely as a dark patch unless seen in favourable light conditions. The two males which spent a whole week in our garden in May, 1980, fed just outside our kitchen window, completely ignoring our son Kevin riding up and down our path on his noisy little tricycle, a mere 10 feet or so from the birds.

The top two birds illustrated are displaying males, seen at Stackhoull trying to impress a female which paid the garden a brief visit in May, 1980.

The centre two illustrations are of a first-year female present around the house in October, 1982. Quite the drabbest I have seen, with no trace of blue at the sides of the throat, a feature present in most females of the species.

The bottom two illustrations are of a first-year male which was present on the isle in September, 1982. The blue was mixed with grey and the whole chin was white. This bird again was most confiding and would run about observers' feet if one waited patiently. Surely a lesson that there really is no need to clap and shout in order to see birds well.

Bluethroats

Red-breasted Flycatcher (4½")

Surprisingly and disappointingly, this species is seldom seen away from the cliffs on the isle, the only inland bird I have seen was in October, 1981. Several have been caught in the Gully trap and a few at the plantation, but allowing for the fact that the Gully, itself a steep-sided ravine, is driven regularly and small birds flushed inland, it is safe to say that on Fair Isle the species really is a cliff-dweller.

I have yet to see an adult male in spring, and in fact have only seen one spring bird (illustrated). Most records of the species are in the autumn, three or four a year being about average. The spring bird was most obliging, flitting about the cliff face at Hesti Geo, but the autumn birds I have seen have not been quite so considerate and the species is surprisingly wary. Fortunately the tail is very conspicuous and birds are relatively easy to locate, even at a considerable distance.

Small, late Wheatears have been mistaken for this species on a number of occasions and it is worth mentioning that these small Wheatears of European origin are often to be seen catching insects in the shelter of buildings and cliffs, very much in the manner of a flycatcher.

A species we had hoped to attract to the garden, but it may be necessary to resort to the telescope and scour the cliffs to add it to our garden list.

Red-breasted Flycatcher

Calandra Lark (7½")

This bird was discovered just as I boarded the plane to go to see Sue, who had just given birth to our son Kevin in Lerwick. Fortunately the bird stayed on the isle for the whole day, and I managed to see it later that evening. It looked rather like a giant Short-toed Lark with a similar dark patch at the sides of the neck. The white tips to the secondaries could be clearly seen as the bird rested on the ground.

Pechora Pipit (5¾")

Almost exclusively Fair Isle's own property in Britain, all but two of the twenty or so records having been here. Late September certainly seems to be the time to see this bird, but none has occurred since we came to Fair Isle to live.

The one I have seen showed the two whitish 'braces' which, unlike the two pale streaks down the back of many other pipits, cut across the back at an angle, rather than going straight up-and-down. The outer tail-feathers were buff, quite different to any of the other small pipits. The underparts were very clean and whitish with bold dark markings. Unfortunately, this individual (September, 1977) was not very vocal, and during the brief opportunity I had to see it, did not call.

Calandra Lark

Pechora Pipit

Red-throated Pipit (5¾")

Although considered to be an extremely skulking species the birds I have seen have been rather more considerate to observers. The spring bird illustrated although seen in long grass at Leogh, flew on to one of the fence-wires where it sat for several minutes allowing excellent opportunities to study its features. The brick-red throat and face was very distinct as were the strongly marked upper parts. The tail was shorter than that of Meadow Pipit and gave the bird a rather squat appearance.

Autumn birds are rather more difficult to identify but the combination of short tail and boldly marked upper parts and, particularly, the 'hissing' call, make the bird distinct from the scores of Meadow Pipits that are on the isle at the time. The call is 'psss', rather like a schoolboy trying to gain someone's attention.

I do not entirely agree with the view that this species is exceptionally elusive and skulking. Having singled out a particularly distinctly marked Meadow Pipit (perhaps a few feathers missing) on several occasions and then endeavoured to re-locate the same individual, I have come to the conclusion that Meadow Pipits are every bit as hard to locate as Red-throated Pipits!

Red-throated Pipit

Tawny Pipit (6½")

One on stoney ground south of the airstrip in June 1978 is the only one of this species I have seen on the isle. A typical spring 'overshoot' record of this large pale pipit which was found on a bright sunny day with south-east winds.

My only previous experience of the species was of a single bird at Holme in Norfolk in the mid-1960's.

Citrine Wagtail (6½")

Well, I'm not convinced about this species. Having seen most of the Citrines recorded at Fair Isle and many autumn Yellow Wagtails showing almost identical plumage and having seen perfectly ordinary Yellow Wagtails giving what is supposed to be a Citrine's call, I find it hard to accept that females and young of each species in autumn are separable.

I have illustrated a typical Citrine with grey upper parts and a pinky-buff wash to the breast, but with the record of a male Citrine pairing with a female Yellow in England a few years ago to add to the confusion, the differences may be less obvious than is at present generally accepted.

Tawny Pipit

Citrine Wagtail

Golden Oriole (9½")

The male illustrated was singing on one of the fence posts near the ringing hut on 29th May, 1980. The female or young male was present near the mast on Ward Hill with another bird in similar plumage on 30th May — 3rd June, 1978.

Woodchat Shrike (6¾")

The young bird illustrated came close, but not close enough, to be added to our garden list. First seen at Upper Stoneybrake, later the Kirk, and finally Midway, a more direct route would have seen it flying right over the shop. Seen on 3rd September, 1980.

Great Bustard (30-40")

Yes, even the Great Bustard is on a few garden lists on Fair Isle!

I spent much of the winter of 1969-70 on the isle and was lucky enough to see the bird both in captivity and in the field.

A Great Bustard feather was found on the isle in 1979, lending weight to my own feelings that, although Fair Isle is small and there may be many birdwatchers present, the number of birds missed must still be quite considerable.

Golden Oriole

Woodchat Shrike

Great Bustard

SPRINGFIELD (derelict) and in background KOOLIN (under construction)

MELVILLE HOUSE (OUTRA) (unoccupied)

Part III

Around the crofts

A contribution from each household
of their own sightings

An illustration of each house accompanies the text

SETTER

One morning in April a few years ago I went into the porch where our son Christopher was playing. A small brown bird had got in somehow and was fluttering against one of the windows. I soon managed to catch it and showed it to Christopher. It was quite pretty, rather like a small streaky sparrow, and I took it outside and let it go. It did look a bit different but not knowing much about birds I thought that it was probably something common.

That afternoon I noticed several birdwatchers in the vicinity, all apparently searching for something. The following day there was even more activity and the Observatory warden's wife came in to tell me that there was a very rare bird in our yard and that attempts were being made to catch it. I mentioned the bird I had caught the previous day and the description seemed to fit the bird they were trying to catch outside. As we chatted over a cup of coffee a knock came on the door. The bird had been caught and was held out for me to see. There was no doubt about it — it was the bird in the porch — a Song Sparrow, all the way from America!

Kathleen Stout

FIELD

To us, birds are part of the scenery and life of Fair Isle and as such are accepted and enjoyed. We may pause in our work to observe a particularly striking bird — and sometimes go as far as to look it up. However, far more interesting are the antics of the birdwatchers, as they try to identify some rarity which is, to us, as drab and uninteresting as a . . . House Sparrow! Once a crowd of binocular-toting persons wanted to follow a particularly intriguing LBJ (little brown job) across the bull's field — very much like a gaggle of penguins: "You go first, and I'll follow if it's safe"! Again, some tried to stalk a little bird across our newly-ploughed field. With eyes glued to binoculars they were stumbling about, unable to see where they were going, and eventually resorted to crawling through the muddy furrows! One young ornithologist patiently and quietly stalked a Hoopoe sitting on our wall — only to find on closer acquaintance that it was my Sunshine Recorder! However, undoubtedly *our* best occasion for twitcher-spotting was when a particularly skulky bird attracted a large following to the skroos at Field. Some thirty "skulked" miserably themselves for ages right outside our porch door — what a splendid opportunity to observe closely the intriguing variety of dress, behavioural characteristics and equipment! Birds and birdwatchers certainly contribute to the fun of living on Fair Isle.

Dave and Jane Wheeler

BARKLAND

One day, the 11th January, 1970, Margaret called me to come and see a "big bird" sitting on the Field Brae. We both agreed that it was a funny looking goose, but could not think what else it could be. It was a foggy day with drizzle and, being the middle of the afternoon, the visibility was not good. However I decided to go and get a closer look. The bird in question was very wary and, as I crept closer, it kept walking from me almost as fast. I was doubled-up, creeping closer and closer and finally got to within 100 yards, when it flew up and quickly disappeared in the fog.

Gordon Barnes, my neighbour at Setter at the time, saw it the following day and, being a keen ornithologist, recognised it at once as a Great Bustard. That same night, I remember, Gordon caught it by dazzling it with a bright light. He kept it in a shed for quite some time, feeding it well, and it was finally sent to Salisbury Plain.

Another interesting bird I remember was the Laughing Gull which spent most of the day flying around our croft on 13th September, 1975.

Alec and Margaret Stout

UPPER STONEYBRAKE

I remember one very strange occurence about fifteen years ago. I was working away at the bench in our shed, when in through the open door flew a bird which landed clean on my shoulder. I turned my head slowly and saw that it was a bonny big Hawfinch. He must have been chased in by a Merlin or other hawk for he sat there for a minute or so just looking at me. Eventually he flew up and sat on a beam at the front of the hay loft. An old tom-cat we kept for catching mice lived up there and the Hawfinch must have woken him up. In a second the bird was in the cat's jaws, just one bite and he was dead. I managed to get the bird from the cat but it was too late. I gave the Hawfinch to Gordon Barnes and he skinned it. I believe he still has it.

A few birds have landed on the Good Shepherd between Fair Isle and Shetland; I remember a Swallow and just a year or so ago we caught a bird on the crossing and the passengers told us it was an Icterine Warbler.

George Stout

SCHOOLHOUSE

It was one quiet sunny day in October of 1982 that there was a sudden interest taken in the Schoolhouse garden. Anyone living on Fair Isle will know that this unusual interest in our garden was not of a botanical nature! During the course of the early afternoon Bill had noticed a tiny bird hopping from one docken weed to another. It was a greenish colour and appeared quite tame. Not being a birdwatcher he did not check the book immediately, and then our two-year-old twins took up his attention and the bird was forgotten.

Later in the afternoon, on the way back from a shopping trip, we were surprised to see a row of binoculars peeping over our garden wall. The excitement was infectious and we soon became involved. Here was a Pallas's Warbler at home in our garden! We had heard of warblers before, but who or what is Pallas? We have since heard of Pallas's Cat — so warblers beware! This tiny bird was a friendly little chap. To the delight of one birdwatcher the bird decided to inspect his shoe and be photographed at the same time! The next port of call was to be my head, but childhood memories of my Budgerigar settling on my head for a purpose came to mind and I'm afraid I moved double-quick!

Elfriede Buchan

LOWER STONEYBRAKE

Rare birds and I don't mix! A few years ago a Bee-eater came to Fair Isle — the day I left for Lerwick! What was probably the same bird then turned up in Lerwick — the day I left Lerwick for Unst!

That event, and the memory of how I managed to miss the Pratincole which spent a whole day at Leogh about the same time, were brought vividly back to me in September 1981 when a beautiful Roller turned up on the isle. This lovely bird spent its time here between the shop yard ('Best for birds,' says John) and our yard ('Best for birds,' says I). I can't remember what I was doing that day, other than that it involved my going up and down the road several times. Ample opportunity to see a Roller, one might think. Not so. Wherever I was, the Roller was somewhere else and in spite of its bright plumage I never did manage to see it!

Does this make me 'King Dipper' I wonder?

I have, however, seen a Great Snipe at the back of the house in 1978 and 1981 and my wife Pat shot a Snowy Owl on the garden wall in April 1979 . . . with her camera!

Neil Thomson

NORTH SHIRVA

In the ten years of our residence on Fair Isle, our family has perhaps been noted more for its ornithological ignorance than for its expertise.

If we had been better informed, we would have known that the handclapping line of men, necklaced with binoculars and cameras, walking beside the ripening grain on an autumn Sunday morning was not a worshipping group conducting its religious rites.

We would have known that it wasn't very funny to tease the assistant warden about our cat having orange feathers sticking out of its mouth when everyone was hunting the Baltimore Oriole in 1974.

Was it the following year when successive birdwatchers were circumnavigating our garden and obviously showing their delight at spotting some rarity? THE bird was a Great Tit and it had been around for several days, giving pleasure as we watched its activities and evoking memories of childhood observations in a Hertfordshire garden. It did not occur to us to tell anyone of this familiar bird's appearance here.

The enthusiasm of both the visitors and the Fair Islanders themselves has over the years stimulated a general interest; we often use the binoculars permanently sited on the work surface near the kitchen window and our bird books are frequently referred to when we share in the excitement of a first or rare sighting.

John and Betty Best

SHIRVA (POST OFFICE)

Some years ago, when I was doing a job of welding, I had cut a short length of three inch pipe and had set it down on the floor of the garage near the door to cool off. I was working on one of the other bits of metal when a small bird suddenly came fluttering in the doorway. After flying around my feet for a moment it disappeared. When I got to the door a Kestrel came swooping down, then darted off twittering angrily. I looked round but could see no sign of the small bird and after a few moments bent down to pick up the piece of pipe. As my hand closed over it the small bird popped out and into my hand. It was a Meadow Pipit. I went out to look around, but the Kestrel had gone so I held the pipit out on my hand and, after a quick look round, it flew off chirping and disappeared round the building.

Early one sunny morning in 1977 we were wakened by a bird singing right outside our bedroom window. We could see the bird with his lovely black-and-white head, singing away merrily, and discovered that it was Britain's first White-crowned Sparrow!

Stewart and Annie Thomson

MIDWAY

I well remember how happy John looked when he called us up to Stackhoull to behold the Roller, but I would also like to have seen his expression if he had stood in his garden as I once did and saw Britain's first Pallid Harrier fly past! It was on the island for several days, and we saw it at Midway, before I obtained it and sent it to the Scottish Museum. Other rarities I have seen from my garden include Eastern Desert Wheatear and White's Thrush, also sent to the above Museum. In October one year I obtained a Calandra Lark at Setter. The specimen was skinned by my father and sent to Paisley's Museum, but unfortunately trace of the said bird went amiss. This was long before the days of the Bird Observatory and the gun was used to prove a very rare bird's identity, and in fact proof of the species was not accepted until it had passed through several expert hands in Edinburgh or London.

I have a midden in my garden, which is a favourite haunt for birds like Bluethroats, particularly on Spring migration. One day however we had another rare visitor to this midden, in the form of a Frenchman! Coming downhill on a cycle he failed to take the bend in the road and landed head-first in the midden — hardly 'eau-de-cologne!!

James Stout

HOULL

I remember when I was small hearing a Corncrake calling in a field of ryegrass, then, after the hay was cut, I was taken to see the young, living in a clump of grass left standing until the birds moved out. After that summer many events have stirred the same feelings, but I will relate only a few of them here. Like taking a yoal into South Ramnageo and seeing the Guillemots pouring off the ledges; or, after searching for hours, to be rewarded by finding a Ringed Plovers nest with four young. The call of the Quail or the noise that a Nightjar makes are a couple of sounds I hope to hear again.

A rare bird is always thrilling to see and the two I remember best were a Shorelark on the hill and a Great Reed Warbler in the hands of Roy Dennis. Another memory from childhood was seeing a Little Auk (Rochie) ashore after a gale. It took a lot of doing to get hold of the little ball of fury and release him back to the sea.

My last word is a hope that the future generations will take the same interest in the birds, and continue to be awed by their beauty and presence.

Brian Wilson

SCHOOLTON

One of my most interesting experiences of a rare bird was the
morning that Ken Williamson, then warden at the Bird
Observatory knocked at the door and asked me "Can you identify
a Pechora Pipit for I'm sure there is one in your cabbages?" My
reply was "I think so if it would only make its call." We went down
to the cabbage patch and at once the small bird flew up making its
call. Right away I said "That is definitely a Pechora Pipit". We
watched it fly around until it landed in the turnip patch at Quoy
and he went across the road to look for it again while I made my
way up to the house with the awful thought in my mind "Have I
made a mistake, is it really what I have said it is?" There wasn't
long to wait until Ken was at the house door again, this time with
the dead bird in his hand. "You were correct," he said and showed
me the markings on its back. No use saying how relieved I was, not
that the bird had killed itself by flying into the telephone wires but
that we now had the proof that it was a Pechora Pipit.

Jimmy Wilson

QUOY

I first became interested in birds when I left school, and settled back in Fair Isle, and over the years I have had many strange encounters with our feathered friends. My croft has one of the few reed-beds on the isle and on one occasion several bird-watchers were trying to identify a bird there. My daughter Mairi who was about three at the time walked up to them and with great aplomb announced 'That's a Quatic warbler'! Other birds seen along the same burn are Marsh, Pallas's, Greenish and Arctic Warblers.

We have seen some of the most impressive birds as well. A Hoopoe which alternated from one end of our tattie-rig to the other as we were lifting tatties. A Snowy Owl sat outside our shed for a while, and the Great Bustard kept us amused a whole morning by pacing along the fence round our cabbages. It didn't occur to him that he could just fly over.

Other birds I have seen and reported are Gyrfalcon, Upland Plover, King Eider and Goldfinch and when I lived with my parents at Shirva I found a Spotted Crake in the byre there.

Stewart Thomson

NORTH LEOGH

When we were young boys we had salt meat or salt fish every day. The men would be off fishing and us boys would try and catch Snow Buntings in the yard. We would have a net in a hoop and prop it up with a stick. When the birds went in to eat the corn we would pull the stick away with the string we had tied to it. The boy who caught one got to eat it. They were small birds but made a fine change.

Some of the older men would make snares from horse-hair and put them on a board and wait for the birds to walk into them. The men would also go round by Sheep Rock in boats and set snares to catch the Guillemots. I believe some of the nails they banged in the cracks in the rocks to hold the snares can still be seen on the skerry near Hesswalls where the Guillemots sit.'

We see many bonny birds, Robins, Wrens, Rock Pipits, and sometimes see the bird-men watching maybe a rare bird along the road.

Willie Eunson

SOUTH LEOGH

In the distant past all rare birds were shot for their skins. Jerome Wilson, Springfield and George Stout, Field were the expert skinners who then submitted them to the Edinburgh museum for mounting and no doubt they can still be seen on show. A few of these birds were cream-coloured, Woodcock, Cormorants and thrushes. In recent years a white Puffin, Cormorant, Starling, Redwing and Shag were observed and left untouched for the bird-watchers to enjoy.

Countless birds of all breeds are now being caught in Heligoland-type traps and herring nets stretched across cropping areas, put into bags then taken to the Observatory to be weighed and ringed.

A worrying aspect of bird-life is the excessive influx of Skuas and Bonxies on the common scattald having a detrimental effect on the economy of the island as there is very little regular employment apart from crofting.

Ever since the inauguration of the Bird Observatory hundreds of visitors have visited Fair Isle, some returning time and time again as they thoroughly enjoy the freedom and goodwill of the community and what a thrill it must be for them to get up in the morning and see a rare bird sitting on a fence post. Early one morning in 1975 we saw a Tennessee Warbler on our fence.

Jerome Stout

BUSTA

I'm ashamed to admit that many of the small, brownish nondescript rarities which fly past my kitchen window don't cause much of a stir, but there are some birds which do compel me to desert duty, grab the glasses and dash outside — a Buzzard perched on the fence post, a Nutcracker sitting on the yellow Land-Rover, a Snowy Owl gazing at me from beside the barn, or the glowing head of a Hawfinch brightening the kail yard.

In September '81 we had a real beauty — a Red-flanked Bluetail. Glancing out of the window I became aware of a head with binoculars attached moving along the edge of the road. Thus alerted, I crept outside very carefully and was rewarded with a close sighting. A true showman, it hopped to within feet of us, showing off its bright orange flanks and the brilliant blue flash of its tail.

One of the few fine days in Dec. '82 I was able to sit on the doorstep and watch a magnificent Gyrfalcon perched on the gable-end of Kennaby. As white as a Snowy Owl, proud and watchful, a royal visitor indeed.

This year hasn't been so exciting. The rarest visitor to the Busta yard so far, 'Gallus gallus domesticus', strayed not from Siberia, I fear, but from Springfield!

Anne Sinclair

SKERRYHOLM

One day I met a 'scarf' in our henhouse — and it wasn't wrapped round a hen's neck! Outhouse doors are traditionally low on Fair Isle and, as I looked up on entering, I saw this 'thing' apparently stretching up to the roof! On closer scrutiny (once my eyes had returned to normal size) I realised it was a 'scarf' or Shag, looking most forlorn. How it came to be there I do not know but I'm sure it was relieved to be taken back to the rocks and lapping waters of the sea-shore, its natural habitat.

Florrie Stout

Here on Fair Isle, man and nature, land and sea all merge, seasons overlap and are recognised by the arrival and departure of the Puffins and the huge falls of migrants, at what is possibly the beginning and ending of summer. During winter storms, as the sea literally overlaps the land, then one may have to stop the car to rescue a Little Auk from off the road, driven inland by the storm. Contrast this to the still of the summer morning, the sun rising from a never dark sky as Fulmars on the chimney welcome the day, always in serious discussion, always striving, at the expense of their neighbour, for a better stance, and drowning out, with their incessant cackle, the song of the lark as it soars and sings to its mate.

James W. Stout

AULD HAA

It was a bit early in the year to be thinking about sweeping chimneys and certainly we'd never discussed it, Bill and I. Still the strong smell in my nostrils was unmistakable and it seemed to emanate from our sitting-room which hadn't been lived in much of late. I was surprised therefore to find a sizeable heap of soot sitting neatly in the grate. It was evident that the mysterious chimney-sweep knew his business. 'God bless Him' I thought. Three nights and many heaps of soot later I had occasion to light the fire. Above the sound of crackling sticks I became aware of a fluttering noise. My first thought was of singed Starlings which do drop in from time to time, but a quick peep up the lum sent me leaping across to Skerryholm for help. James William, sensing the situation donned thick gloves and armed himself with a large stick. Soon the bird was in the hand, thankfully not mine, since I was suffering from an acute attack of the 'Hitchcock Horrors'!

Now if you should see our sweep gliding past your chimney you will most likely mistake him for a Fulmaris glacialis 'dark phase', but you'd be wrong for in fact he is another 'First for Fair Isle' — Fulmaris DOMESTICUS — and we hope that he'll become a regular visitor!

Margo Murray

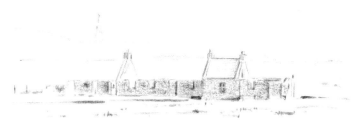

PUND (ruin)

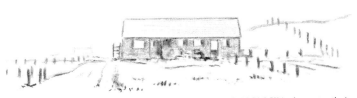

SHELTERED HOUSING BLOCK (under construction)

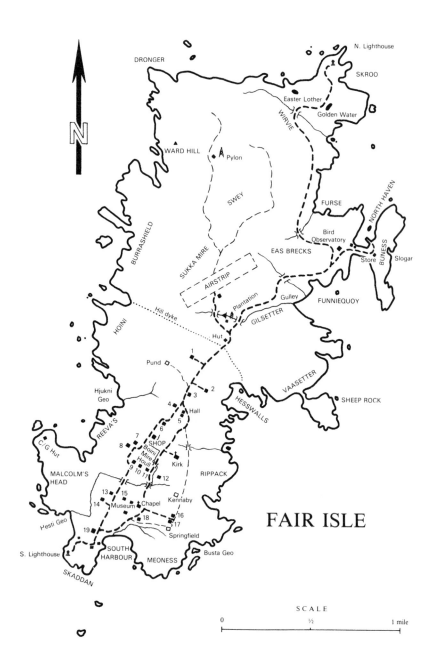

KEY

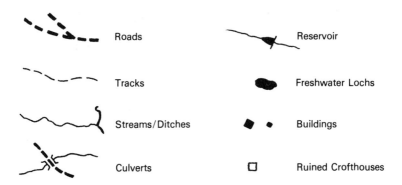

Roads

Tracks

Streams/Ditches

Culverts

Reservoir

Freshwater Lochs

Buildings

Ruined Crofthouses

Index to Dwellings

1 Setter
2 Field
3 Barkland
4 Upper Stoneybrake
5 Schoolhouse
6 Lower Stoneybrake
7 North Shirva (nurse's)
8 Shirva (Post Office)
9 Midway
10 Houll

11 Schoolton
12 Quoy
13 North Leogh
14 South Leogh
15 Taft
16 Busta
17 Skerryholm
18 Auld Haa
19 Outra

ACKNOWLEDGMENTS

A special thank you to the Fair Islanders who have all allowed me access to their land, a privilege I have very much appreciated. A thank you too for their encouragement and assistance with this book.

A thank you to the Fair Isle Bird Observatory who have given me access to records and their skin collection, and to Nick and Liz Riddiford who have always alerted me whenever a 'rary' has turned up.

A thank you to my wife Sue, who gave up all claim to rights at the kitchen table while this book was in production, and to Dave Davenport, Tony Hulls and Mike Witherick for their comments on the original text.

And finally, a thank you to the many visitors to the isle who have helped to make *our* birdwatching enjoyable.

J. F. Holloway

INDEX

Bee-eater 78
Blackbird 12
Blackcap 34
Bluetail, Red-flanked 120
Bluethroat 46, 122
Brambling 24
Bullfinch 64
Bunting, Black-headed 38, 112, 114
  Cretzschmar's 110, 114
  Lapland 40, 114
  Little 80, 114
  Ortolan 76, 110, 114
  Pallas's Reed 70, 114
  Pine 108, 114
  Red-headed 58, 114
  Reed 20, 114
  Rustic 50, 114
  Snow 12, 114
  Yellow-breasted 106, 114
  Yellow-browed 104, 114
Bustard, Great 132
Buzzard 44
  Honey 70
  Rough-legged 82

Chaffinch 22
Chiffchaff 36, 90
Coot 44
Cormorant 40
Corncrake 68
Crane Sandhill 66
Crossbill 52
Crow, Hooded 12
Curlew 18

Diver, Great Northern 82
Dove, Collared 32
  Rock 14
  Turtle 32
Duck, Ring-necked 42
Dunlin 58
Dunnock 22

Eider 56

Fieldfare 14
Flycatcher, Pied 26
  Red-breasted 124
  Spotted 34
Fulmar 12

Gannet 18
Godwit, Bar-tailed 36
Goosander 76
Goldcrest 26
Goldeneye 44
Goose, Barnacle 38
  Bean 38
  Greylag 40
  Pink-footed 18
  White-fronted 62
Greenfinch 26
Greenshank 38
Guillemot 68
  Black 68
Gull, Black-headed 20
  Common 20
  Glaucous 14
  Great Black-backed 14
  Herring 14
  Iceland 64
  Lesser Black-backed 20
Gyrfalcon 84

Harrier, Hen 36
  Marsh 76
Hawfinch 30
Heron 42
Hobby 48
Hoopoe 62

Jackdaw 18

Kestrel 18
Kite, Red 42
Knot 78

Lapwing 16
Lark, Calandra 126
  Short-toed 62
Linnet 36

Mallard 42
Martin, House 32
  Sand 36
Merganser, Red-breasted 40
Merlin 16
Moorhen 56

Nightingale 118
  Thrush 118

Oriole, Golden 132
Ouzel, Ring 24
Owl, Long-eared 56
  Short-eared 32
  Snowy 58
Oystercatcher 18

Peregrine 38
Pigeon, Wood 18
Pipit, Meadow 18
  Olive-backed 82
  Pechora 126
  Red-throated 128
  Richard's 38
  Rock 14
  Tawny 130
  Tree 26
Plover, Golden 16
  Grey 70
  Ringed 16
Pochard 42
Puffin 24

Quail 78

Rail, Water 64
Raven 14
Razorbill 58
Redpoll 30
  Arctic 56
Redshank 22
  Spotted 52
Redstart 26, 119
  Black 22
Redwing 12
Robin 12
Roller 72
Rook 20
Rosefinch, Scarlet 54
Ruff 24

Sanderling 80
Sandpiper, Buff-breasted 60
  Green 30
  Wood 66
Shag 12
Shelduck 44
Shrike, Great Grey 20
  Isabelline 74
  Red-backed 32
  Woodchat 132
Siskin 56
Skua, Arctic 30
  Great 24
Skylark 16
Snipe, Common 16
  Great 72
  Jack 16
Sparrow, House 12
  Song 116
  Tree 66
  White-throated 116
Sparrowhawk 34
Starling 14
Stonechat 18
Swallow 30
Swan, Whooper 24
Swift 34
  Alpine 68

Teal 44
Tern, Arctic 48
  Common 52
  Sandwich 50
Thrush, Mistle 22
  Song 12
Turnstone 14
Twite 16

Wagtail, Citrine 130
  Grey 58
  Pied 20
  Yellow 46
Warbler, Aquatic 96
  Arctic 92
  Barred 54
  Garden 36
  Grasshopper 44
  Great Reed 102
  Greenish 90
  Lanceolated 100
  Marsh 48
  Melodious 94